The Hidden Key to Management

Table of Contents

Introduction 3

Chapter 1: Understanding the Spectrum of Control 5

Chapter 2: The Footsteps That Came Before 8

Chapter 3: Key Features of Strong Leadership 24

Chapter 4: Hiring Practices 37

Chapter 5: Common Challenges 46

Chapter 6: Cover your back. 59

Chapter 7: Tips 62

Chapter 8: Great Senior Leaders 66

Introduction

"The line separating good and evil passes not through states, nor between classes, nor between political parties either—but right through every human heart." – Alexander Solzhenitsyn.

When I first embarked on my journey as a manager, I was armed with the belief that the right strategy and clear goals were the ultimate keys to success. I mapped out plans with precision, confident that this was the path to leading my team to success. However, as I traversed the complex terrain of leadership, I encountered challenges that strategy alone could not overcome. It was in these moments of struggle that I began to sense that something crucial was missing.

No matter how meticulously I planned, there was a void in my approach—a lack of depth that left me yearning for a more profound connection with my team. I realized that true leadership was not merely about directing others towards a destination; it was about inspiring and empowering them to embark on their journeys with passion and purpose.

This feeling of incompleteness is not unique to my experience. Many managers, despite their best efforts, find themselves grappling with the same elusive piece of the puzzle. They achieve success in measurable terms yet feel a sense of disconnection and unfulfilled potential.

Leadership, I discovered, is not just about the external goals we set, but also about the internal voyage we undertake. It is about understanding our own strengths and weaknesses, cultivating empathy and authenticity, and creating an environment where each team member feels valued and inspired. It is a journey that requires us to look beyond the surface, to dive deep into the essence of what it means to lead with both head and heart.

In this book, we will explore these hidden keys of management—those often-overlooked elements that can transform good managers into great ones. We will delve into the stories and experiences that illuminate the path to true leadership, uncovering the profound insights that lie beneath the surface of traditional management wisdom. Together, we will embark on a journey of discovery, seeking to unlock the full potential of ourselves and those we lead.

Chapter 1: Understanding the Spectrum of Control

Before we can delve any further, we need to understand the difference between what you can and cannot control, it is a vital skill. Understanding this balance is akin to mastering a delicate dance, where each step is crucial to leading a successful team.

The Sphere of Influence: Your Direct Actions

Controllable factors are those within your reach, where your actions and decisions can make a tangible impact. These are the elements you can shape with intent and effort.

• Personal Conduct: Your attitude, work ethic, and approach to challenges are entirely within your control. Like a diligent gardener tending to their plants, your consistent care and attention can cultivate a thriving work environment.

• Team Dynamics: While you cannot change each person's intrinsic nature, you can influence the atmosphere in which they work. By setting clear expectations, fostering respect, and encouraging collaboration, you can create a harmonious and productive team dynamic.

• Strategic Decisions: Planning projects, allocating resources, and setting goals fall under your sphere of influence. Approaching these tasks with careful analysis and foresight ensures that your decisions are well-founded and effective.

The Unpredictable Elements: Beyond Your Reach

Uncontrollable factors are those external elements that you cannot directly influence. Recognizing these and learning to navigate them is essential for effective management.

• External Environment: Market trends, economic shifts, and regulatory changes are beyond your control. However, staying informed and adaptable allows you to respond to these changes proactively, turning potential threats into opportunities.

• Human Behaviour: The actions and decisions of others, whether stakeholders, competitors, or team members, can be unpredictable. Understanding human nature, practicing empathy, and maintaining flexibility can help you manage these uncertainties with grace.

• Random Events: Unforeseen circumstances, such as natural disasters or sudden technological disruptions, are inevitable. Developing robust contingency plans and fostering a resilient mindset within your team prepares you to handle these events effectively.

While the distinction between controllable and uncontrollable factors is clear, their interaction is where skilled management truly shines. By focusing on what you can control, you enhance your ability to influence what you cannot. For instance, a well-prepared team (controllable) can better adapt to unexpected market changes (uncontrollable).

Practical Strategies for Managers

• Set Clear Priorities: Focus on areas where your actions will have the most significant impact. Delegate tasks effectively and empower your team to take ownership of their responsibilities. Truly and deeply understand what your team does to ensure you can set realistic deadlines and goals. If your staff are leaving work late every day, that's not a good thing!

• Develop Resilience: Encourage a mindset of growth and adaptability within your team. Provide training and resources to help them cope with change and uncertainty.

• Foster Open Communication: Create an environment where information flows freely. Transparency helps in managing expectations and building trust, essential for navigating uncontrollable factors. Knowledge is power—empower your staff.

- Embrace Continuous Learning: Stay updated with industry trends and innovations. A commitment to lifelong learning equips you with the knowledge to anticipate and respond to external changes effectively.

- Lead by Example: Demonstrate the behaviours and attitudes you wish to see in your team. Your actions set the standard, fostering a culture of integrity, hard work, and dedication. Show your team that you are committed to the same principles you expect from them.

Chapter 2: The Footsteps That Came Before

In my career, I had the privilege of working under seven different managers. Each of them brought unique strengths, weaknesses, and leadership styles to the table. Reflecting on their approaches offers valuable insights into the diverse ways leadership can manifest and the impact it can have on a team.

Manager 1: The Former Musician

My first manager was a musician in the UK grime industry who had worked with notable names such as Ed Sheeran. Coming from humble beginnings, he avoided micromanagement and instead gave us the freedom to work as we saw fit. Our work involved helping at-risk youth, including young offenders and distressed families. His leadership style, rooted in trust and autonomy, showed me that giving people the freedom to act independently can lead to creativity and empowerment, especially in tricky situations.

In my time working with this manager, I uncovered critical principles of people management:

• Integrity is Fundamental: Keeping promises and being a person of your word builds trust, regardless of age or status.

• Respect is Essential: Addressing everyone with respect and recognizing their value enhances cooperation and morale.

• Effective Crowd Management: In situations where you're outnumbered, managing the crowd takes precedence over conventional customer service.

From my manager, I learned the importance of preparation, innovation, and communication:

• Preparation: Starting the day early and preparing thoroughly sets a strong foundation for success. Good preparation and planning will enhance your ability to influence what you cannot control and minimize potential risks and hazards.

• Innovative Spirit: Embracing new ideas and approaches can lead to significant improvements and breakthroughs. The routine tasks and daily grind can become repetitive and dull, but injecting creativity and trying new methods can transform mundane activities into engaging and enjoyable experiences. By fostering a culture of innovation, we can not only enhance efficiency and productivity but also boost team morale and make the work environment more dynamic and stimulating. Encouraging employees to think outside the box and experiment with novel solutions can uncover hidden potentials and drive the organization forward in unexpected and exciting ways.

- Clear Communication: Ensuring that all team members are informed and aligned fosters unity and efficiency. When everyone is on the same page, misunderstandings and errors are minimized, leading to smoother operations and a more cohesive team dynamic. Transparent and consistent communication helps build trust, encourages collaboration, and ensures that everyone is working towards the same goals. Regular updates, open channels for feedback, and clear directives help maintain focus and streamline efforts, making it easier to address issues promptly and keep projects on track. By prioritizing clear communication, we create an environment where every team member feels valued and informed, ultimately enhancing overall productivity and success.

Manager 2: The Saint

My second manager was a mature lady who often told me I was the age of her children. Despite being underqualified and inexperienced, she gave me my big break into a better-paying job in the housing industry. She saw my genuine drive and desire for growth and believed in my potential.

The role was as an income officer in the housing industry. Most of my encounters, about 9 out of 10, were negative due to the nature of the job. In my first month, she knew I was struggling, but instead of berating me she made sure I was ok, that I was taking my breaks and eating my lunch when I didn't feel like it. This manager taught me that you cannot punish someone that is already giving 110% but still failing but instead give them time and mentorship. She made sure I got some extra training, tried different methods of training and alas I broke the hidden glass barrier that was stopping me for getting my stride. Remember when it comes to learning/training there isn't a one shoe fits all solution - that's lazy.

In this position, I learned that you can't end every interaction positively, the customer is not always right, and no matter how difficult the workday was, you need to separate your work life from home life to avoid bringing negativity home and affecting your loved ones.

This was one of my all-time favourite managers and she taught me so many wonderful things about dealing with people in an office and more importantly negative environment:

• Give People a Chance: Recognize and nurture potential in others, even if they lack experience or qualifications. Remember, if someone hadn't given you a chance, you wouldn't be in the very position you are in now.

• Control Your Volume: Maintain a calm and composed demeanour, especially in challenging situations. Sometimes, in an argument, you may need to raise your voice, but often the smartest thing to do is to lower it. When you speak more quietly, the other party will have to lower their volume as well if they wish to hear you. If they have no intention of listening, they are not trying to communicate but rather choosing to pick a fight. In such cases, disengaging is wise to conserve your energy. Use the modulation of your volume to your advantage.

• Know the Line: Understand and respect the boundaries between professional and personal life to maintain a healthy work-life balance. Remember that workplace disputes with customers or colleagues are professional issues, not personal attacks, and should be treated as such. However, it is crucial to respect your boundaries. If comments are made with ill intent that have nothing to do with work, they should not be tolerated. Maintaining this balance ensures a respectful and productive work environment.

Additionally, knowing the line involves being able to switch off from work mode when you leave the office. Carrying the stress of your workday into your personal life can harm your relationships and mental health. It's important to establish routines or activities that help you decompress and transition into your personal time, whether it's through exercise, hobbies, or spending quality time with loved ones. This separation is key to sustaining long-term well-being and happiness.

Manager 3: The DJ

My third manager, also in the housing industry, had seen the great work I was doing and handpicked me for a more senior position on his team. He was the youngest of all my managers and brought a dynamic, energetic approach to leadership. With a background in DJing, he had a knack for reading the room and adjusting his style to fit the needs of his team. He was also finishing a degree in accounting by attending university in the evenings. He was a master of balance, knowing when to push for more and when to let things flow naturally. His leadership style combined high energy and adaptability, always keeping the team motivated and engaged.

Although this role was very admin heavy, I further developed my knowledge of housing, but the most important take away for me was understanding the true value of workplace relationships.

With increased responsibility, I learned the importance of networking and building relationships. Establishing strong connections within and outside the organization made my job easier and allowed me to fast-track solutions for clients. Networking helped me navigate the complexities of my role more efficiently, provided valuable support, and opened new opportunities for growth and advancement.

Manager 4: The One Still Polishing His Oxfords

My fourth manager presented a dynamic I had never encountered in the workplace before. Some might consider me fortunate to have had smooth and supportive relationships with previous managers, each fostering a conducive environment for growth and collaboration. However, this new scenario was starkly different.

Transitioning from the housing industry to a Qatari-owned real estate, lettings, and development company, I found myself under the purview of a manager who, while an exceptional doer, struggled significantly with coordination. His dedication to the senior team was evident and, in many ways, commendable. However, the friction between us arose from our mutual bluntness and honesty. Unlike my predecessors, he was not inclined to nurture or mentor, a stark contrast to my ambition and hunger for career progression.

My requests for increased responsibilities were often met with resistance. His blatant favouritism and reluctance to allow me room for growth were concerning, as they threatened to stunt my professional development. This manager's lack of empathy was particularly striking. I vividly recall him dismissing a colleague's mental health concerns with the harsh proclamation, "Everyone claims to have mental health issues; if you're not diagnosed, you're not ill." His discriminatory attitudes towards sexual orientation and religious practices further exacerbated workplace tensions. Denying staff days off for religious holidays, insisting only one member could take leave such as days as Eid, led to internal strife and a fractured team dynamic.

However, a turning point arrived when his favoured female employee left the department three months later. Needing to delegate her responsibilities, he began to rely on me more, leading to a gradual improvement in both our professional relationship and my role within the team.

This was a fast-paced environment and nevertheless this manager did end up teaching me many great things related to data analysis, project management and stakeholder relationships. But the key transferable lessons for me would be that the place of work can be unpredictable with steady waves turning into a tsunami so, work smart not hard. Create shortcuts that do not compromise quality and automate as much as you can - technology is your friend.

But in terms of management skills, I have witnessed many things from this manager which I knew when I was given an opportunity, I would do different:

• Value Everyone: Never make someone feel like they have no value. A leader who fails to recognize and acknowledge the worth of their team members sow seeds of discontent and disengagement. In any organization, every individual plays a crucial role, and it is the leader's responsibility to ensure that each person feels appreciated and significant. By recognizing the unique contributions of each team member and expressing genuine appreciation, a leader can cultivate a motivated, loyal, and high-performing team. This approach not only enhances morale but also fosters a culture of mutual respect and collaboration, driving the organization towards greater success.

• Open-Mindedness: Give things you don't understand a chance. Embrace new ideas and perspectives to uncover potential for innovation and growth. This openness fosters a culture of curiosity and adaptability, driving creative solutions and broadening horizons.

• Conscious of Bias: Be aware and conscious of bias in all forms. We all have biases, but it's crucial to keep them in check. Recognize and address your own biases to ensure fairness and equity.

• Proactive Training: Train people proactively rather than as a last resort. Effective training should be a continuous process, not a reactive measure. Implement a proactive training plan that anticipates the skills and knowledge your team will need in various scenarios. Ensure that all team members are well-prepared and capable of handling any challenges that may arise. By investing in proactive training, you enhance overall performance, build confidence, and reduce the likelihood of errors in critical situations.

Remember, preparation through consistent training is key to achieving operational excellence and success.

• Avoid Conflict: While friendly competition can be beneficial, do not pin people against each other. Creating an environment of direct competition among team members can lead to hostility and a toxic work atmosphere. Instead, foster a culture of collaboration and mutual support. Encourage teamwork and collective problem-solving to achieve common goals. Healthy competition should be balanced with cooperation to maintain a positive and productive work environment. By avoiding divisive tactics, you can build a cohesive team that works together effectively.

Manager 5: The Peter Principle

Due to a company restructure, I took it upon myself to speak to my manager and director as my team was facing reductions. Part of me disliked the feeling of instability at my job, and another part of me simply wanted to try something new. I was informed about a position at our sister organization, which specialized in housing in the private sector this time. In comparison to the public sector, this really did feel like a walk in the park. With the exorbitant prices they charged clients, the organization ensured that each building had an engineer, cleaner, concierge, and security guard—sometimes multiple in the larger buildings.

So why was this the worst job I had ever done?

The main reason was the toxic work environment created by the manager's behaviour.

First, consider the nature of taking credit for others' work while swiftly blaming others for mistakes, often in public. This behaviour not only demoralizes the team but also erodes the trust and cohesion essential for a functional workplace. When standards and rules change unpredictably, it creates an unstable environment where employees are perpetually on edge, unsure of what is expected of them. Worse yet, when attempts to seek clarification are met with gaslighting, it undermines confidence and discourages initiative.

This manager also exhibited a generally hostile attitude, shifting from a friendly demeanour to aggressive outbursts with both staff and customers. This volatility made the work environment exceptionally stressful. Despite being warned that employees typically left within six to nine months, I joined the team, perhaps hoping I could withstand the storm.

The practical aspects of the job were equally mismanaged. We were given limited lunch breaks, insufficient uniform supplies, delayed overtime pay, and were forced to work additional hours without proper compensation. The manager's favouritism was blatant; she would waste time chatting with her preferred employees, then complain about her workload to the rest of us.

Her insecurity and lack of competence were glaringly evident. She once accidentally locked a customer in the basement due to improper handling of digital locks, leading to customer berating of staff. Despite instructing us to consult her when unsure, she would redirect us to outdated manuals and then gaslight us when things inevitably went wrong.

Perhaps one of the most egregious examples was when she instructed a driver to exceed the legal passenger limit on a caddy, and subsequently blamed the driver when this directive caused issues. This type of leadership is not only inefficient but downright dangerous, fostering a culture of fear and mistrust.

• Respect for Adults: Treat employees as adults who have their own lives and responsibilities outside of work. Managers should avoid demeaning behaviour that makes employees feel like children. Respect is fundamental to a productive and positive workplace environment.

• Lead by Example: As a manager, it's crucial to have a deep understanding of the job and the business. You cannot effectively lead or teach others if you don't have comprehensive knowledge yourself. Leading by example sets a standard of excellence that inspires and guides your team.

• Accountability: True leadership involves taking full responsibility for your actions and decisions. Blaming others undermines trust and erodes morale within the team. Holding oneself accountable fosters a culture of honesty and integrity.

• Recognition and Support: Acknowledge and celebrate the achievements of your team members. Instead of taking credit for their work, give them public recognition. This not only boosts their morale and confidence but also demonstrates your leadership by highlighting the team's accomplishments. Supporting and championing your team builds loyalty and a sense of camaraderie.

Manager 6 & 7: The First Mate & The Captain

Knowing my self-worth, I left my former venture and moved decided to move forward with my life and career. I was back in square one but this time I have experience on myside.

I joined a Fortune 500 company, and this was the largest company I had ever worked for. They once said that the sun never sets on the British empire, well the sun also never sets on this company, with offices in the States, Latin America, parts of Europe, Africa, Asia and I wouldn't even be surprised if they launched a branch on the moon next.

In this organisation I had two co-Managers, managers 6 &7, represented two contrasting approaches to leadership that complimented each other. This may have been one of the first time I had seen two managers work so closely without trying to outshine each other and what was the outcome? They shined brighter. Working under them provided yet another unique perspective on how different management styles can impact team dynamics and productivity.

Manager 6 embodied a leadership style characterized by approachability, honesty, and a friendly demeanour. They fostered a work environment where team members felt valued and appreciated.

They were approachable and easy to talk to, creating an open-door policy that encouraged team members to voice their opinions and concerns. This accessibility-built trust and facilitated effective communication within the team.

They kept transparency in their interactions, providing honest feedback and guidance to help team members improve their performance. Their sincerity and straightforwardness contributed to a culture of trust and accountability.

They had a knack for boosting morale with humour and positivity. They celebrated team successes by surprising us with treats like ice cream and cake, fostering a sense of camaraderie and motivation. This recognition of our efforts reinforced our commitment to achieving team goals.

Rather than micromanaging, they empowered the team to take ownership of their work. They trusted our capabilities and only intervened when necessary, allowing us the autonomy to innovate and excel in our roles.

- Trust and Empowerment: Have trust in your team members and empower them to take initiative.

- Positive Culture: Their emphasis on humour and rewards showed me how positive reinforcement can enhance team morale and performance and is much more effective than a negativity or mistake-based leadership when the manager is then viewed in a much darker light leading to loss of respect and lack of approachability.

- Open Communication: By fostering open communication and transparency, Manager 6 created a supportive environment where everyone felt heard and valued.

Manager 7 oversaw the office with a vigilant and distant yet supportive leadership style. Their approach combined authority with compassion, ensuring a productive and respectful work environment.

She maintained a vigilant presence, overseeing the office operations with a keen eye for detail and efficiency. Their leadership was akin to a captain guiding a ship, ensuring that the team stayed on course towards achieving goals.

While not hesitant to hold team members accountable for their actions and decisions, Manager 7 never resorted to belittling or demeaning anyone for mistakes. Their feedback was constructive, aimed at fostering growth and improvement rather than criticism.

She showed empathy towards team members' well-being. They understood the challenges of mental health and emphasized the importance of taking sick days not only for physical illness but also for mental well-being. Their supportive approach created a culture where team members felt valued and understood.

- Respectful Authority: Manager 7 taught me the balance between authority and empathy, maintaining respect while ensuring accountability.

- Compassionate Leadership: Their understanding of mental health issues and support for taking sick days underlined the importance of prioritizing well-being in the workplace.

- Professional Oversight: Like a captain overseeing a ship, Manager 7's distant yet vigilant leadership style ensured operational efficiency and goal attainment while fostering a supportive team environment.

Summary

- Integrity and Respect: Uphold integrity by honouring commitments and showing respect for every individual's contribution, fostering a cooperative and motivated team environment.

- Effective Management: Prioritize crowd control and thorough preparation to mitigate risks and ensure smooth operations, mastering the art of proactive planning.

- Innovative Communication: Embrace innovative communication strategies to inspire creativity and streamline processes, ensuring clarity and alignment among team members.

- Empowerment and Conflict Resolution: Recognize and nurture potential in others while keeping composure during challenging situations, effectively managing conflicts to uphold a harmonious work-life balance.

- Networking and Bias Awareness: Cultivate strong networks and remain vigilant against biases, promoting fairness and inclusivity within the workplace culture.

- Proactive Leadership and Team Dynamics: Proactively train and develop team members, encouraging collaboration and teamwork over competition to foster a positive and productive work environment.

- Respectful Leadership: Lead by example with comprehensive knowledge and accountability, earning respect through consistent integrity and exemplary conduct.

- Recognition and Empowerment: Celebrate achievements openly and empower team members to take initiative, building loyalty and camaraderie through genuine appreciation.

- Positive Influence and Communication: Maintain a positive leadership style with humour and open communication, nurturing morale and supporting mental well-being while ensuring operational efficiency.

Chapter 3: Key Features of Strong Leadership

Communication

Clear and precise communication is essential for effective leadership as it sets up order, reduces misunderstandings, and builds trust within a team. Leaders who communicate effectively ensure that their team understands goals, expectations, and any changes that occur, fostering a stable and productive work environment.

When it comes to communication, it is crucial to understand that it is only 7% verbal, 38% vocal, and 55% visual. This means that 93% of communication is non-verbal. Therefore, what you say is the least important part of communication. Leaders must be very conscious of their vocal tones and how they appear visually.

Practical Non-verbal communication tips:

• Be Mindful of Your Tone: Pay attention to how your tone of voice might be perceived. Practice speaking in a calm, clear, and confident manner.

• Facial Expressions: Your facial expressions can significantly affect how your message is received. Smiling can convey friendliness and openness, while frowning can indicate displeasure or disapproval.

• Use Positive Body Language: Ensure your body language is open and approachable. Avoid crossing your arms or displaying other closed-off postures.

• Maintain Eye Contact: Use eye contact to show you are engaged and attentive. This can help in building stronger connections with your team.

• Timing and Pacing: The timing and pacing of your responses can affect how your communication is perceived. Rushed responses can seem impatient, while well-timed pauses can convey thoughtfulness.

Practical verbal communication tips:

• Positive and Encouraging Language: Using positive language can boost morale and motivation within your team. Focus on what can be done rather than what cannot. Instead of saying "We can't do that," say "What we can do is..." Use words that inspire confidence and optimism, such as "achieve," "improve," and "opportunity."

• Dealing with someone stubborn: My rule of thumb when dealing with stubborn people is to lead with two positive compliments on what we are doing well before mentioning what we can do better. This usually prevents them from hurting their ego and makes them feel more secure.

• Clear and Concise Language: Being clear and concise helps prevent misunderstandings and ensures your message is understood. Avoid using unnecessary jargon or complex terms. Break down complex ideas into simpler components. Use short sentences and be direct. Always ask yourself could I explain this to a child and have them understand it? If the answer is yes, that's the standard.

• Empathetic Language: Empathetic language shows you care about your team members' perspectives and feelings. Acknowledge others' emotions and viewpoints with phrases like "I understand how you feel," "That sounds challenging," or "I appreciate your perspective."

• Open-Ended Questions: Open-ended questions encourage dialogue and deeper thinking. Instead of asking yes/no questions, ask questions that require more detailed responses, such as "What are your thoughts on...?" or "How do you feel about...?"

• Constructive Criticism: Constructive criticism helps improve performance without demoralizing team members. Frame feedback in a way that focuses on improvement. Use the "sandwich" method: start with positive feedback, then provide criticism, and end with encouragement.

By being conscious of both verbal and non-verbal aspects of communication, leaders can significantly enhance their ability to lead effectively. Clear and precise communication, complemented by strong non-verbal cues, not only establishes order and reduces misunderstandings but also builds a foundation of trust and respect within the team.

Approachability

Approachability is a critical trait for effective leadership. When leaders are approachable, team members feel comfortable sharing ideas, concerns, and feedback. This openness fosters a safe space, positive work environment, enhances collaboration, and leads to better problem-solving and innovation. Approachability helps build trust and respect, which are essential for maintaining strong, cohesive teams.

Key Benefits of Approachability:

• Enhanced Communication: When leaders are approachable, team members are more likely to communicate openly and honestly. This openness leads to the free flow of ideas. Imagine a team where every member feels confident to share their wildest ideas without fear of ridicule—this is where groundbreaking solutions and revolutionary projects are born.

• Increased Trust & Higher Engagement: An approachable leader builds a foundation of trust and mutual respect. This trust is the bedrock of a loyal and committed team. When employees trust their leader, they are more likely to go above and beyond, showing dedication and resilience even in challenging times. Approachability boosts morale and creates an energetic, positive work environment. Engaged employees are not just present—they are passionate, driven, and committed to their work. This heightened engagement leads to higher productivity, lower turnover, and a workplace buzzing with enthusiasm.

• Avoiding the "Yes Men" Phenomenon: Leaders who are not approachable often find themselves surrounded by "yes men"—individuals who agree with everything the leader says rather than offering honest feedback. This environment stifles innovation, hides potential problems, and leads to poor decision-making.

Strategies for Being More Approachable

- Open-Door Policy: Physically and metaphorically open your door to your team. Make time for informal conversations and be genuinely available for your team members. Show them that you are there to listen and support.

- Active Listening: Focus on the speaker, maintain eye contact, and provide feedback that shows you are engaged. Summarize or paraphrase their points to confirm understanding. Demonstrating that you value their input encourages more open communication.

- Non-Judgmental Attitude: Respond to all input with an open mind. Avoid making snap judgments or dismissive comments. Show appreciation for their honesty, even if you disagree with their point of view.

- Transparency: Be open and honest about your decisions, plans, and the reasons behind them. Share relevant information with your team and explain the rationale behind your decisions. Transparency helps build trust and ensures everyone is on the same page.

- Regular Check-Ins: Schedule regular one-on-one meetings with team members to discuss their progress, concerns, and feedback. Use these meetings to build rapport, address any issues, and show that you care about their well-being and professional development.

- Celebrate Wins: Offer praise and recognition both publicly and privately. Celebrate team successes and individual accomplishments to show appreciation and boost morale.

- Be Approachable in Digital Spaces: Ensure your approachability extends to virtual interactions. Use friendly and welcoming language in emails and messages. Be responsive to communications and use video calls to maintain a personal connection when working remotely. Take advantage of emojis, as you cannot share tone or emotion through text, emojis are a great substitute.

- Personal Connection: Show interest in your team members' lives outside of work. Ask about their interests, hobbies, and families. Share appropriate personal stories to create a sense of camaraderie. Remember details about their lives and follow up on them.

Approachability is a vital aspect of effective leadership that fosters a positive, open, and trusting work environment. By implementing strategies such as maintaining an open-door policy, practising active listening, demonstrating empathy, being transparent, using positive body language, scheduling regular check-ins, celebrating wins, being approachable in digital spaces, and building personal connections, leaders can create a more inclusive and supportive atmosphere. This not only enhances team morale and engagement but also drives better collaboration and innovation, leading to overall organizational success.

Emotional Intelligence

Leaders with high emotional intelligence have been found to create a 20% better team performance compared to those with low EI, according to research by the Hay Group.

Key Components of Emotional Intelligence:

- Self-Awareness
- Self-Regulation
- Motivation
- Empathy
- Social Skills

The Fascinating Benefits of Emotional Intelligence

- Improved Decision-Making: Leaders with high Emotional Intelligence can better understand and manage their emotions, leading to more rational and effective decision-making. By staying calm and focused, they can assess situations objectively and make decisions that benefit the entire team.

- Enhanced Relationships: Emotional Intelligence helps leaders build stronger, more meaningful relationships with their team members. By understanding and empathizing with others' emotions, leaders can create a supportive and collaborative work environment where everyone feels valued.

- Effective Conflict Resolution: Leaders with high Emotional Intelligence are adept at managing conflicts. They can navigate disputes by understanding the underlying emotions and addressing them constructively. This skill transforms potential conflicts into opportunities for growth and improved team dynamics.

- Resilience: Emotional Intelligence equips leaders with the resilience needed to cope with challenges and setbacks. By managing their own emotions and helping their team do the same, they can maintain a positive outlook and steer the team through difficult times.

• Increased Retention: High Emotional Intelligence in leaders contributes to a positive work environment where employees feel understood and valued, leading to increased job satisfaction and retention rates. Retaining top talent saves the organization significant costs associated with turnover and recruitment.

Strategies for Developing and Utilizing Emotional Intelligence

• Developing Self-Awareness: Reflect on your emotions and understand how they impact your behaviour and decisions. Keep a journal to track your emotional responses and identify patterns. Seek feedback from trusted colleagues or a mentor to gain insights into your strengths and areas for improvement.

• Practising Self-Regulation: Learn to manage your emotions by practising mindfulness and stress-reduction techniques. When faced with a challenging situation, take a moment to pause and breathe before responding. Develop strategies to remain calm and composed under pressure.

• Cultivating Motivation: Implementation: Set personal and professional goals that are meaningful and challenging. Maintain a positive attitude by focusing on your accomplishments and progress. Inspire yourself and others by demonstrating enthusiasm and commitment to your work.

• Building Social Skills: Develop strong communication and interpersonal skills. Practice active listening, clear articulation, and effective non-verbal communication. Foster a collaborative environment by encouraging open dialogue and teamwork. Work on building rapport with team members and stakeholders.

Emotional Intelligence is a vital component of effective leadership. By developing self-awareness, practising self-regulation, cultivating motivation, enhancing empathy, and building social skills, leaders can harness the power of Emotional Intelligence to improve decision-making, build stronger relationships, resolve conflicts effectively, boost team morale, and enhance resilience. Incorporating these practices into your leadership style will create a more supportive, productive, and successful work environment.

Professional Vs Personal

While we often emphasize the importance of maintaining professionalism in the workplace, it's crucial to acknowledge that work is inherently personal for everyone involved. Every decision, every interaction, and every outcome can have significant personal implications for employees. Understanding and balancing the professional and personal aspects of leadership is key to fostering a supportive and empathetic work environment.

The Fascinating Interplay Between Professional and Personal

- Decisions Impact Lives: Every professional decision, from project assignments to promotions, and especially terminations, impacts employees on a deeply personal level. A manager might say, "It's not personal, it's just professional," but for the employee facing job loss, it is profoundly personal. They worry about their financial stability, their family, and their future.

- Empathy in Leadership: Recognizing the personal implications of professional decisions is crucial. Leaders who demonstrate empathy and understanding can better support their team members through difficult times. Empathetic leadership builds trust and loyalty, as employees feel valued and understood beyond their job roles.

- Long-Term Benefits of Compassionate Leadership: Compassionate leadership has long-term benefits. Employees are more likely to stay with a company where they feel personally valued and supported. This reduces turnover, enhances team stability, and creates a culture of mutual respect and loyalty.

Strategies for Balancing Professional and Personal:

- Communicate with Compassion: When delivering difficult news or making tough decisions, approach the conversation with empathy. Acknowledge the personal impact on the employee and offer support where possible. Also, give them time to process the news or update, don't rush them.

- Be Transparent and Honest: Be open about the reasons behind your decisions and the challenges the organization is facing. Transparency helps employees understand the professional context and reduces the sense of arbitrary decision-making.

- Encourage a Work-Life Balance: First, let's acknowledge most people work for money and have no interest or genuine passion for their job. They work because they have to, they spend 40 hours or more a week with you and probably see you more than their real families, I think that's enough and making sure they have personal space and also time to rest and recover is key. Promote policies that support work-life balance if possible, such as no contact outside of working hours, flexible working hours, remote work options, and encouraging employees to take their holiday days and sick days.

- Recognize Personal Achievements: Acknowledge and celebrate personal milestones, such as birthdays, weddings, a birth of a child, and personal achievements. This recognition shows that you see and value your employees as whole individuals, not just workers.

Examples of Balancing Professional and Personal Boundaries

- Example 1: Imagine a workplace where the manager takes the time to remember and celebrate each team member's birthday. On these special days, the manager brings in a cake, and everyone gathers to sing and celebrate. This small but meaningful gesture shows employees that they are valued as individuals, not just for their work contributions. It fosters a sense of belonging and community, making the workplace feel more like a supportive family. Such moments create lasting memories and strengthen the bond between team members and their managers.

- Example 2: A leader who encourages team members to take time off when needed and supports flexible working arrangements shows respect for their personal lives. This balance leads to happier, more productive employees who feel their well-being is prioritized. Remember not everything can wait till after work or the weekend, these days even the bank closes by 5 PM.

Balancing professional and personal boundaries is essential for effective leadership. While maintaining professionalism is crucial, recognizing and respecting the personal aspects of work can lead to a more empathetic, supportive, and productive work environment. By communicating with compassion, showing genuine interest, being transparent, offering support during transitions, encouraging work-life balance, and recognizing personal achievements, leaders can foster a culture that values both professional excellence and personal well-being. This approach not only enhances team morale and loyalty but also drives long-term organizational success.

Slow is Smooth & Smooth is Fast

The principle "Slow is Smooth, Smooth is Fast" is rooted in the understanding that taking the time to do things correctly and thoughtfully leads to better, more efficient outcomes in the long run. This can be applied when training new staff, implementing new protocols or even learning and developing to become a manager yourself.

In leadership, this approach emphasizes the value of patience, thoroughness, and deliberate action. By focusing on quality and careful planning, leaders can ultimately achieve faster and more sustainable results.

- Importance of Patience and Precision: Taking the time to plan and execute tasks carefully ensures that the foundation is solid. Rushing often leads to mistakes that require additional time and resources to fix. By being patient and precise, leaders can ensure that projects start on the right foot and progress smoothly.

- Preventing Mistakes and Rework: A deliberate approach helps in identifying potential issues early on, allowing for corrective measures before they escalate. This prevents costly mistakes and the need for rework, ultimately saving time and resources. Doing it right the first time often means not having to do it again.

- Building Sustainable Success: Sustainable success comes from consistent and thoughtful effort. Leaders who adopt a "Slow is Smooth, Smooth is Fast" mindset prioritize long-term goals over short-term gains, ensuring that their actions have a lasting positive impact on the organization.

Strategies for Implementing "Slow is Smooth, Smooth is Fast":

Thorough Planning: Spend adequate time in the planning phase of projects. Clearly define goals, outline steps, allocate resources, and anticipate potential challenges. Involve your team in the planning process to ensure comprehensive coverage and buy-in.

Pacing Projects: Break down projects into manageable tasks and set realistic deadlines. Avoid overwhelming your team with tight schedules. Instead, promote a steady, sustainable pace that allows for thoughtful execution and adjustment as needed.

Regular Check-Ins: Schedule regular check-ins with your team to monitor progress and address any issues early on. Use these meetings to review milestones, provide feedback, and make necessary adjustments to stay on track.

The principle "Slow is Smooth, Smooth is Fast" underscores the importance of patience, precision, and deliberate action in leadership. By focusing on thorough planning, prioritizing quality, pacing projects, conducting regular check-ins, encouraging reflection, and promoting a culture of patience, leaders can achieve more efficient and sustainable results. This approach not only prevents mistakes and rework but also builds a strong foundation for long-term success, enhances team cohesion, and fosters a positive work environment.

☐

Chapter 4: Hiring Practices

In the ever-evolving landscape of business, the foundation of any successful organization lies in its people. Hiring the right talent is not just about filling positions; it's about strategically building a team that embodies the company's values, drives innovation, and contributes to a positive and productive work environment. Effective hiring practices are the bedrock of organizational success, influencing everything from company culture to long-term growth. This chapter delves into the intricacies of the hiring process, offering insights and strategies to attract, evaluate, and retain top talent in a competitive market.

Strategic hiring

Strategic hiring goes beyond just matching resumes to job descriptions. It's about understanding the long-term goals of the organization and identifying candidates who not only have the required skills but also align with the company's mission and values. The right hire can propel a team forward, fostering innovation and driving performance, while a poor hiring decision can lead to discord, decreased productivity, and increased turnover.

There are several methods organizations can use to hire employees. Here's a detailed breakdown of the various hiring methods that you can use:

• Direct Hiring: Involves the organization managing the entire hiring process internally. This method allows for greater control over the selection process, ensuring the candidates align closely with the company's culture and requirements. However, it can be time-consuming and resource intensive.

• Recruitment Agencies: Can be valuable partners in the hiring process, especially for specialized or high-volume hiring needs. Agencies have extensive networks and expertise in sourcing and screening candidates, which can expedite the hiring process and provide access to a broader talent pool.

Using a recruitment agency over an internal hiring team can offer several advantages despite the potential drawbacks. Recruitment agencies have extensive networks and databases of candidates, often reaching a wider and more diverse talent pool than an internal team. They can tap into passive candidates who are not actively seeking new opportunities but might be a perfect fit for the role. They are also known to fill positions more quickly than internal teams because they are dedicated solely to recruitment. They have streamlined processes, existing candidate pipelines, and the resources to conduct thorough searches efficiently.

However, the downside to this is agencies may prioritize quantity over quality to fill positions quickly. This can result in a higher turnover rate if the placed candidates are not well-suited for the roles.

- Employee Referrals: Leveraging existing employees to refer candidates is a highly effective hiring method. Employee referrals often lead to higher quality hires who are a good cultural fit, as employees are likely to recommend individuals they believe will succeed in the organization.

Referral programs can be incentivized to encourage participation. Referred employees typically have higher retention rates compared to those hired through other methods. They are more likely to stay with the company longer, as they often have a clearer understanding of the company culture and expectations through their referrer. Also, Employee referral programs can reduce recruitment costs and reduces the risk of making poor hiring decisions, as employees are unlikely to refer individuals who they do not believe will succeed in the role.

While employee referrals offer numerous advantages, they also come with significant drawbacks that organizations must carefully manage. One major concern is the lack of diversity; employees often refer individuals who are like themselves in background and perspective, which can lead to a homogenous workforce and limit the variety of ideas and experiences that are crucial for innovation and problem-solving. Another issue is the potential for nepotism, where employees might refer friends or family members regardless of their qualifications, resulting in favouritism and undermining the merit-based hiring process. This can erode trust in the recruitment system and demoralize other employees. Furthermore, the use of employee referrals can lead to strained relationships within the workplace. If a referred candidate is not hired or fails to perform well, it can create tension between the referring employee and their colleagues or supervisors, potentially disrupting team dynamics and negatively impacting workplace morale. Therefore, while employee referrals can be a valuable recruitment tool, it is essential to balance them with other hiring methods to ensure a diverse, fair, and harmonious work environment.

- Internships and Apprenticeships: Internships provide a valuable opportunity for companies to gain additional support in a cost-effective manner. By bringing on interns, businesses can benefit from the fresh perspectives and enthusiasm of students and recent graduates while managing budget constraints, as interns typically receive lower compensation compared to full-time employees. This arrangement allows companies to tackle specific projects or alleviate workloads during busy periods without significant financial investment. Moreover, internships offer a mutually beneficial arrangement, where businesses not only gain extra hands but also contribute to the professional development of young talent. Interns gain practical experience, build their professional networks, and develop essential skills that enhance their future employability. These programs are beneficial for both the organization and the candidates, as they offer practical experience and an opportunity for the company to assess potential long-term employees.

• Job Fairs: Recruiting events are excellent for hiring recent graduates and young professionals. These events provide a platform to engage with a large number of candidates in a short period, allowing for on-the-spot interviews and assessments.

• Online Job Portals and Career Websites: Utilizing online job portals and the company's career website is a standard practice for reaching a wide audience. Job portals like LinkedIn, indeed, and Glassdoor can help attract diverse candidates, while a well-designed career page can highlight the company culture and benefits, appealing to potential hires.

While online job portals and career websites offer various advantages, there are several reasons why they might be considered the least effective method of recruitment compared to other approaches such as employee referrals, recruitment agencies, or direct hiring through company networks.

These platforms often result in fewer candidates applying as they lack external advertising, and the user experience can be cumbersome and unfriendly. Additionally, the impersonal and generic nature of the application process fails to capture the specific nuances of both the company's culture and the job role, making it difficult to assess a candidate's true fit. Furthermore, there is a risk of candidates providing false or exaggerated information, necessitating thorough and time-consuming background checks.

These issues collectively make online job portals less effective compared to more targeted and personalized recruitment methods.

• Gig Platforms and Freelancers: For temporary, project-based, or highly specialized work, hiring freelancers or gig workers through platforms like Upwork, Freelancer, or Fiverr can be a viable option. This method provides flexibility and access to a global talent pool.

You will also need to make sure you post an accurate Job Description.

A well-crafted job description is the first step in attracting the right candidates. It should be clear, concise, and compelling, providing a realistic preview of the role and the expectations. Key components include:

• Job Title and Summary: Clearly state the job title and provide a brief overview of the role.

• Responsibilities: Outline the primary duties and responsibilities, highlighting how the role contributes to the organization.

• Qualifications: Specify the required education, experience, skills, and any preferred attributes.

• Company Overview: Share a snapshot of the company's mission, values, and culture to attract candidates who resonate with these aspects.

• Call to Action: Encourage potential candidates to apply by providing clear instructions on how to submit their application.

The Interview Process

Interviews are a critical component of the hiring process, offering a chance to evaluate a candidate's fit beyond their resume. Effective interviews should be structured and consistent, ensuring each candidate is assessed fairly. Key strategies include:

• Behavioural Questions: Focus on past behaviour as an indicator of future performance by asking candidates to describe specific situations and their responses.

• Skill Assessments: Use practical tests or assignments to evaluate the candidate's technical abilities and problem-solving skills.

• Cultural Fit: Assess how well the candidate aligns with the company's values and work environment through questions about their work style and preferences.

• Panel Interviews: Involve multiple team members in the interview process to gain diverse perspectives on the candidate's fit.

• Diverse Perspectives: Encouraging diversity in hiring to bring in a variety of perspectives and ideas, fostering innovation and creativity.

• Dynamic Interview Questions: Regularly change and refresh interview questions to ensure candidates cannot rely on scripted answers, allowing for a more genuine assessment.

During the interview process, it's important to look beyond the surface and identify key traits and behaviours that indicate a candidate's potential for success within your organization. While technical skills and specific knowledge are essential, it's crucial to remember that skills can be trained, but character cannot. Here are critical areas to focus on:

Onboarding for Success

The hiring process doesn't end with an accepted offer. Effective onboarding is essential to integrate new hires into the organization and set them up for success. A comprehensive onboarding program should include:

- Introduce new hires to the company culture, policies, and procedures.

- Provide the necessary training to equip new employees with the tools and knowledge they need to perform their roles effectively.

- Assign mentors or buddies to help new hires navigate their new environment and build connections.

- Regularly check in with new hires to gather feedback and address any concerns, ensuring a smooth transition and early identification of potential issues.

Retaining Top Talent

Retaining top talent begins with the hiring process but extends throughout the employee's tenure. Foster a supportive and engaging work environment by:

• Providing Opportunities for Growth

• Recognizing and Rewarding performance incentives to motivate and retain employees.

• Promoting Work-Life Balance: Support employees in supporting a healthy work-life balance through flexible work arrangements and wellness programs.

Mastering the art of hiring is a continuous journey that requires attention to detail, strategic thinking, and a genuine commitment to building a strong, cohesive team. By implementing effective hiring practices, organizations can attract and retain the talent needed to drive innovation, achieve their goals, and maintain a competitive edge in the market remember to make it your own experience and don't be afraid to try something new. This chapter has provided a comprehensive guide to navigating the complexities of the hiring process, ensuring that each new addition to the team contributes to the organization's success.

☐

Chapter 5: Common Challenges

Gaining Respect and Establishing Authority

New managers often struggle to gain respect and establish their authority within a team, especially if they were promoted from within the team or are significantly younger or less experienced than their subordinates.

Competence is the bedrock of respect. To gain respect and establish authority, new managers must demonstrate a high level of competence. This involves continually developing both technical and managerial skills. Focus on mastering the necessary knowledge and skills pertinent to your role. When team members see that you are competent and knowledgeable, they are more likely to respect your decisions and leadership.

You must also demonstrate ethical behaviour and honesty; this is crucial for establishing authority. Lead by example by being transparent, reliable, and honest in all your interactions. Admit mistakes when they occur and consistently act in accordance with your values and principles. This fosters trust and shows your team that you are a dependable leader.

Take responsibility for your actions. Assuming responsibility rather than avoiding it is key to establishing authority. Hold yourself accountable for your decisions and the performance of your team. Address issues directly and proactively solve problems. Don't be afraid to call them out if they are doing anything wrong but also understand and empathize with them too. Make sure you give people a chance to explain things, it is too easy to assume and jump to conclusions. If ever approached make sure you listen to their concerns, recognize their individual strengths and challenges, and provide support where needed. This relational approach fosters trust and respect.

Lasty and most importantly, give your team time to adjust. Transitioning to change such as a new manager can be challenging for both the manager and the team. Show patience and understanding as your team adapts to your leadership style and expectations.

Time Management and Delegation

With great power comes great piles of paperwork and an overbooked calendar.

If you are managing for the first time, you must remember that you are moving away from individual work and stepping into the realm of genuine teamwork. Being a manager is about coordinating a team or department and ensuring everything flows smoothly.

Take a moment to ask yourself, "If everything that could go wrong did go wrong, but I only have the resources to fix one thing, what would I fix?" Then expand this to two things, three things, and so on. By questioning yourself in this way, you gain a clear understanding of what your priorities are. This process helps ensure that you are focusing your time on activities that have the greatest impact on your team's success.

Plan for the Unplannable. Keep time slots free throughout the day. Ensure you're not going from meeting to meeting without a break. Allocate free time slots to handle unexpected issues that may arise and to connect with your staff. This flexibility allows you to address unforeseen challenges and maintain a presence with your team.

There's no such thing as a one-man army. The company has given you staff to use appropriately. Delegate tasks strategically by understanding the strengths and weaknesses of your team members and assigning tasks that align with their skills and development needs. Delegation is not just about offloading work but also about empowering your team. Provide clear instructions and expectations and ensure that team members have the necessary resources and authority to complete their tasks.

Also, make sure you leverage productivity tools. Use project management software, calendar apps, and other digital tools to keep track of tasks, deadlines, and team progress. These tools help you stay organized and ensure nothing falls through the cracks. With communication platforms like

Microsoft Teams and Slack, you can easily ask questions and share information without wasting time walking to the other side of the office.

Managing Conflict

Managing conflict is an inevitable part of being a manager. Handling disagreements and disputes effectively is crucial for maintaining a positive work environment and ensuring team productivity. There are different types of conflicts which we will explore.

Manager vs. Manager

Conflicts between managers can occur due to differences in strategic direction, resource allocation, or management styles. If involved in a dispute with another manager, it is important to keep the conflict private as it helps maintain a professional atmosphere within the organization. Staff may lose respect for either manager if they witness conflicts, which can undermine authority and credibility.

To prevent and minimize these conflicts, encourage direct communication between the managers involved to understand each other's perspectives. Setting up a private meeting where all parties can express their views and concerns without interruption is crucial. Do not bottle things up; expression is healthy. Additionally, acknowledge different jurisdictions within the organization, respect their boundaries, and set yours. This helps in maintaining clear lines of responsibility and authority.

If things continue to escalate, consider involving a higher-level manager or HR to mediate the conflict and provide an unbiased perspective. A neutral third party can facilitate a productive discussion and guide the managers towards a resolution. By keeping conflicts private, encouraging open communication, respecting boundaries, and seeking mediation, when necessary, managers can effectively resolve disputes while maintaining a professional and respectful workplace.

Manager vs. Employee

Conflicts between a manager and an employee can arise due to misunderstandings, differences in expectations, communication breakdowns, or perceived unfair treatment. Effectively managing these conflicts is crucial to maintaining a positive work environment and ensuring team productivity.

When conflicts arise between a manager and an employee, it is essential to address the issues promptly and constructively. Start by actively listening to the employee's concerns and acknowledging their feelings. This demonstrates respect and helps in understanding the root cause of the conflict. Avoid being defensive and focus on finding a fair solution.

Clear communication is key. Ensure that roles, responsibilities, and expectations are explicitly communicated and understood by both parties. Misunderstandings often stem from ambiguous instructions or expectations, so taking the time to clarify these aspects can prevent many conflicts.

Providing constructive feedback is also crucial. Offer feedback that is specific, actionable, and focused on improvement rather than criticism. This helps the employee understand areas for development without feeling attacked. Additionally, be open to receiving feedback from the employee, as this can provide valuable insights into their perspective and foster a more open and trusting relationship.

Involve the employee in finding a resolution. Encourage them to share their ideas on how the situation can be improved and be willing to make necessary adjustments. This collaborative approach not only helps in resolving the current conflict but also empowers the employee and strengthens their engagement with the team.

If the conflict persists or escalates, it may be necessary to involve HR or a higher-level manager to mediate the situation. An impartial third party can provide an unbiased perspective and help facilitate a fair resolution.

If an employee from a different team approaches you with concerns about their manager, it's important to handle the situation with sensitivity, fairness, and professionalism. Ensure the employee feels comfortable sharing their concerns by providing a private, confidential setting. Listen without interrupting, showing empathy and understanding to demonstrate that their concerns are taken seriously. Make sure you fully understand the situation by asking open-ended questions that encourage the employee to provide more detailed information. Avoid making immediate judgments or taking sides; maintain a neutral stance to ensure a fair assessment of the situation.

Remember, the way you handle this information has the potential to either damage or strengthen relationships with the employee and their manager. Take the information with pinch of salt, recognizing that it could be based on lies or misunderstandings. Ask the employee if they would be comfortable involving HR, and if they agree, involve HR to ensure that the appropriate policies and procedures are followed. Note that these guidelines apply to minor disputes. Any serious allegations, such as physical abuse, racism, homophobia, or discrimination, must be reported without exception, as there can be no tolerance for such behaviour in the workplace.

Employee vs. Employee

Conflicts between employees are common in the workplace and can stem from misunderstandings, competition, differences in work styles, or personality clashes. Effectively managing these conflicts is crucial to maintaining a positive work environment and ensuring team productivity. Here's how to handle employee vs. employee conflicts:

It's essential to address conflicts as soon as they surface to prevent escalation. Early intervention can stop misunderstandings from developing into larger disputes. Arrange a confidential meeting space where both employees can express their concerns without fear of judgment or retaliation. This helps create a secure environment for open dialogue.

Listen attentively to both parties involved. Allow each employee to explain their perspective without interruption, showing empathy and understanding to demonstrate that their concerns are taken seriously. Encourage the employees to communicate directly with each other to resolve their issues, if possible.

Encourage the employees to work together to find a mutually beneficial solution. Collaboration can lead to more effective and lasting resolutions and strengthen working relationships. Be cautious of forced solutions, as they can leave internal resentment and issues unaddressed, leading to repeated conflicts. If the conflict cannot be resolved through direct dialogue, consider involving a neutral third party, such as HR or a mediator, to facilitate a resolution.

If you are the mediator, make sure to document the details of the conflict and the agreed-upon resolution. This ensures clarity and accountability and provides a reference if the issue resurfaces. Check back with the employees to ensure that the resolution is effective and that the conflict does not reoccur. Continuous monitoring can help maintain a harmonious work environment.

Finally, make sure to give both parties time to cool off. This might mean keeping them away from each other physically or not assigning them tasks where they need to interact.

Understanding Team Dynamics

Understanding team dynamics is essential for any manager aiming to lead a cohesive and high-performing team. Team dynamics refer to the invisible forces that influence the relationships and interactions among team members. Recognizing and effectively managing these dynamics can significantly impact your team's productivity, morale, and overall success. You must remember unless you are building a team from scratch you are going into a pre-existing team with a pre-existing status quo and relationships. You might be tempted to want to implement changes but its key to understand these dynamics before trying to improve things. A mechanic doesn't mess with random parts he evaluates a car first.

Firstly, observe and assess your team. Spend time understanding the individual personalities, work styles, and strengths of your team members. Pay attention to how they interact with one another, both in formal meetings and informal settings. Identify any patterns of behaviour, such as who tends to take the lead, who prefers to follow, and how decisions are made within the group. This observational phase will provide you with valuable insights into the underlying dynamics at play.

Promote open communication as it is the cornerstone of healthy team dynamics. Encourage team members to voice their opinions, share their ideas, and express their concerns. Its best to lead by example so you should be the one to start these conversations initially to let them know these are acceptable topics to openly discuss.

Leverage diversity within the team. A diverse team brings a variety of perspectives, skills, and experiences, which can lead to more innovative solutions and better decision-making. Someone younger or less experienced is not a week link, rather someone with a fresh prospective. I love getting new employees involved with providing feedback regarding big discussions. Why? Because they haven't aligned themselves with the views of their piers yet. Their opinions are often raw and honest. And if they have no idea what you're asking them it means the subject of the conversation has been made over complicated, if you cannot explain something to someone with no knowledge and have them understand it, this is a huge sign you've gotten side tracked and need to go back to the basics. Remember big or complicated isn't always better, sometimes it's unnecessary. Simple can be better.

Establish clear roles and responsibilities. Ambiguity can lead to confusion and inefficiency. Ensure that each team member understands their role, responsibilities, and how they contribute to the team's goals. Grow the team by having them shadow each other so they can be cross functional. Also make sure you understand the roles and responsibilities, there is nothing more awkward for an employee then being told to do a task outside of your job spec. Clear expectations help prevent overlap, reduce conflicts, and increase accountability.

Monitor team dynamics regularly. Team dynamics are not static; they evolve over time as team members join or leave and as the team faces new challenges. Regularly assess the health of your team's dynamics and be proactive in addressing any issues that arise. Use tools such as team surveys, feedback sessions, and performance metrics to gauge how well your team is functioning.

Building Confidence

Confidence is a critical attribute for effective management, impacting various aspects of leadership and organizational success. A manager's confidence not only influences their personal performance but also affects the overall morale and productivity of their team.

Confidence is integral to leadership and decision-making. A manager who exudes confidence is more likely to make decisions swiftly and assertively. This decisiveness is essential in a fast-paced business environment where delays can lead to missed opportunities and setbacks. Confident managers trust their judgment and are willing to take calculated risks, which can lead to innovative solutions and competitive advantages. Furthermore, confidence allows managers to set a clear vision and direction for their team.

Effective communication is another area where confidence plays a pivotal role. Managers need to convey ideas, expectations, and feedback clearly and persuasively. Confidence enables managers to articulate their thoughts in a manner that is authoritative, engaging and approachable. This clarity in communication helps prevent misunderstandings and ensures that everyone is on the same page. Moreover, confident managers are good talkers and storytellers which makes people want to listen to them. They are also better listeners, as they are not preoccupied with self-doubt or insecurity.

In times of crisis, confidence becomes even more vital. During challenging periods, employees look to their leaders for guidance and reassurance. Seeing a confident manager can instil confidence in the team. Their confidence can mitigate panic and maintain focus on finding solutions. This ability to lead effectively under pressure not only helps in resolving the immediate crisis but also strengthens the team's confidence in their leader for future challenges.

The best way to boost your confidence is by knowing your product and team inside out, knowledge is power. Besides how can you be proud or even defend a team or product if you don't understand it yourself.

Take time to self-reflect. Think deeply about you're concerns, worries and regrets, write them down and think about what you can learn from them. You cannot change past experiences but if we are afraid of a particular issue we can prepare for it, preplan solutions for it and acknowledging your concerns, worries and regrets should reduce yourself doubt leading to more confidence.

Lastly, outside of work you can engage in regular physical activity. Exercise improves your physical health and releases endorphins, which can enhance your mood and confidence.

Work life balance.

Achieving a healthy work-life balance is essential for maintaining overall well-being, productivity, and job satisfaction. This balance also helps slow down staff burnout, including your own.

If you are not on call, make sure you stick to your working hours. Avoid working outside of these hours unless absolutely necessary. Unless you work remotely, you should never be taking work home with you physically or mentally. There is no reason for work to contact you outside of your working hours unless it's an absolute emergency. Unless you are a manager, if it is an emergency, the company should only be calling managers, the police, the fire department, or an ambulance. An employee being asked to work outside of their hours is a sign of poor planning. As a manager, it should rarely come to this, if at all.

Be realistic with tasks. Prioritize important tasks and come back to less important ones later. If there is too much on your plate, perhaps it's time to speak to your managers and ask for additional resources. There is no point in constantly working late yourself or overworking staff; it's demoralizing, unhealthy, and will lead to burnout.

Chapter 6: Cover your back.

"*Men judge generally more by the eye than by the hand, because it belongs to everybody to see you, too few to come in touch with you.*" - Niccolò Machiavelli.

In the workplace, this means that appearances and perceptions often hold more weight than the unseen efforts behind the scenes. To protect your reputation and credibility, ensure that your actions appear genuine, transparent, and in alignment with company standards. Most importantly, make sure they paint you in a positive light. This ensures that others judge your actions favourably, granting you more support and allies in the work environment.

You never truly realize how many eyes are on you. Sometimes it's sheer luck. Sometimes it's people who look up to you, and unfortunately, sometimes it is people looking for your downfall. When I first started, I must admit it was from a place of pure laziness, but then it turned into a routine for me. I would often, and very randomly, leave a single lace untied. From this, I noticed how many people would stop me to tell me, including close colleagues and complete strangers like the cleaner. Now, it's safe to assume, if all those people saw and spoke to me, then there must have been those who didn't see or saw and didn't care.

When people saw and spoke to me, it showed their attentiveness and care. They noticed details and took the time to inform me, whether they were close colleagues or complete strangers like the cleaner. Their willingness to speak up indicated a proactive nature and respect for my well-being, even over something as small as an untied shoelace.

Those who did not speak can be categorized into two groups: those who saw and did not speak, and those who did not see. Those who saw but said nothing might have done so out of indifference or discomfort. They noticed but chose not to mention it, possibly to avoid awkward interactions or simply because they did not care. Their silence could also stem from being too focused on themselves or lacking the confidence to speak up. On the other hand, those who didn't see at all were likely focused on their own tasks or thoughts, causing them to overlook such details. They might prioritize different aspects of their environment, paying attention to what they deem more important. This group's lack of awareness indicates a gap in their situational perception, possibly due to distraction, disinterest, or simply being in a hurry.

One takeaway from this is that the ones who notice your lace being undone are those you should trust more with responsibility. It can be hard to distinguish who has seen and not spoken up compared to someone who genuinely did not see, so pay extra attention to those who do speak up. You need to genuinely understand the traits of your team to manage and bring the best out of them.

As a manager, it's crucial to protect yourself and your decisions to maintain credibility and prevent potential issues. "Covering your back" means taking steps to ensure accountability, that your words and actions cannot be manipulated against you, and that correct documentation is in all relevant places. Let's explore the strategies that will help you cover your back effectively.

First, document everything. In the vast landscape of corporate life, detailed records of meetings, decisions, and communications are your map and compass. Emails, memos, meeting minutes, and reports—all these create a clear trail of actions and rationales. They are invaluable when disputes arise or when you need to defend a decision. After important discussions, follow up with a written email. This confirms that everyone is on the same page, ensuring clarity and preventing misunderstandings.

Second, have witnesses and double-check with upper management. Involve a third party as a witness when making significant decisions or having crucial conversations. A colleague, HR representative, or another manager can serve this role. Having witnesses helps validate your actions and provides additional perspectives. For major decisions or changes, confirm with upper management. Seek written approvals to ensure that your actions are authorized and supported. This not only protects you but also ensures alignment with the company's strategic direction.

Lastly, follow company policies and procedures. Familiarize yourself with your organization's guidelines. Make sure every action and decision you take aligns with these standards. Consistently adhering to company policies protects you from accusations of favouritism or rule-breaking. When in doubt, seek advice from HR or senior management. Their guidance provides an extra layer of security and approval for your decisions.

☐

Chapter 7: Tips

• Study people - take the time to learn about your colleagues and peers. Strive to know everyone personally by learning at least three key things about each person. First, understand their professional background—their role, experience, and expertise. This helps you appreciate their contributions and know whom to turn to for specific insights or assistance. Second, discover their personal interests and hobbies. Knowing what they enjoy outside of work can provide common ground for building rapport. Third, learn about their motivations and goals—what drives them in their career and what they aspire to achieve. This knowledge allows you to support their ambitions and align your interactions in ways that are mutually beneficial. Ironically some people will only care about the pay check but that's ok.

• Control the options - Although the workplace can often feel like a dictatorship with managers dictating tasks, this method of management typically breeds resentment. Key performance indicators (KPIs) and targets are often set without much room for negotiation, leaving employees feeling powerless. To mitigate this, it's crucial to make employees feel like they have a choice in their tasks. When faced with a task that people are reluctant to do, present them with options. Frame the necessary task as the most attractive option among a few choices. For instance, if a tedious report needs to be completed, you might offer it alongside even less appealing tasks or suggest different approaches to the task that give them some control. By doing so, employees feel a sense of ownership and autonomy, transforming ingratitude into gratitude as they perceive the decision as their own.

• Work on the hearts and minds of others: Be valued by your team by making them feel valued and engaged. In the short term, fear is a toxic but useful motivational tool, but it will lead to resentment, workplace enemies, and employees looking to leave. That's why I prefer to lead with love. Leading from a place of love, compassion, and understanding may not always give you short-term success, but it will give you long-term success. When you make people feel like you are looking after them, they are much more likely to get the job done—sometimes to make you proud and sometimes simply to avoid making you look bad in front of your managers. They are also more likely to pay attention to detail, care more about their job, burn out less, and stay with the organization longer, giving you a steady but slow momentum for success. If everyone you train leaves for a less toxic workplace, you'll find more work on your shoulders, essentially going back to square one often.

To work on the hearts and minds of others, give them time; it's that simple. Giving employees time and building rapport with them is key. When they trust you, they will tell you what is going on at home or what is concerning them that you may be able to help with. For example, if you find that an employee had to skip lunch to run some errands on their break, perhaps it's worth letting them have some extra time to grab some food. A well-fed employee is a hard-working employee.

• Preach the need to change, but never reform too much at once: Change, especially positive change, is a great way to improve things. However, it's crucial to implement these changes slowly for success. Change of any sort can be an uphill battle, with many clinging to old ways. Implementing changes gradually gives employees time to understand the reasons behind them, increasing their acceptance and commitment. It also ensures that the transition is smooth and minimally disruptive. Gradual implementation allows you to backtrack if a change is miscalculated, with minimal disruptions. Additionally, slow transitions reduce the risk of overwhelming employees and causing disruptions to daily operations.

• Ask for feedback: Never assume—just ask. Many things can go wrong, but it's how we fix them that matters. We should always focus on maintaining a growth mindset rather than a negative one. Often, you will notice something is wrong when employees come into work looking fatigued or if there is high turnover. Even if you think you know the cause, it's always better to ask for feedback.

Seeking feedback allows employees to feel heard and ensures that you confirm the issue before attempting to fix it. Many employers overlook their employees' needs, such as hiring more staff to manage the workload or conducting salary reviews to match the cost of living and inflation, opting instead for superficial solutions like pizza parties. Your employees are not children—a £10 pizza will not help them with their workload or paying their rent.

- Combine Old and New Knowledge: There's nothing that will give you more of an edge than combining the knowledge of the old and the new. Old knowledge tells us what works based on data, wisdom, and general experience. New knowledge teaches us how to work smarter, not harder. It offers fresh perspectives, especially when something is outdated. It's about automation, using the right software to save money, and efficiently managing and analysing data through tools like Microsoft Excel or Google Sheets.

For example, as an income officer, we used to have software that provided a list of all properties in debt needing contact. Managing over 5,000 properties, with almost 1,000 of those properties owing money, the software aimed to organize our process of contacting tenants. However, with incoming calls, admin tasks, and court dates, contacting 1,000 tenant's weekly was impossible. The software would reset weekly, often causing us to revisit accounts unnecessarily, while lower debt cases were neglected due to prioritization of high debt cases.

A new manager introduced a spreadsheet with debt information broken down from highest to lowest. By dividing up the calling campaign and eliminating the need to check the same accounts repeatedly, our productivity soared, and debt levels dropped significantly. Following this success, we ended our contract with the special software company and found Excel to be far more useful.

- Creating emotional highs and lows: If nothing changes, everything stays the same. It's important to create emotional highs and lows in the workplace. When your team or a specific employee does something great, celebrate it.

Give them a shout-out, praise, and a well-deserved pat on the back. It's the least you can do, showing you appreciate them and are proud of their achievement. Let them be an example to others, setting the standard for excellence. If you do not reward above-and-beyond effort, why should anyone do more than the bare minimum for basic pay?

• With the highs come the lows. People sometimes miss targets, make mistakes, or, like my friend Aladdin, accidentally swear in an interview—as the interviewer. The most important thing to remember is that, in most cases, we are not dealing with life or death. Mistakes happen, and we need to learn from them and even be able to laugh at them. However, we also need to hold ourselves accountable. Depending on the frequency and severity of the mistakes, this might range from explaining the errors to more serious conversations.

• When it comes to addressing mistakes, never publicly humiliate anyone. Telling someone off in front of their colleagues is humiliating and can severely damage their confidence. Always address such issues privately.

Chapter 8: Great Senior Leaders

Don Vultaggio, *co-founder and CEO of Arizona Beverages*

Don Vultaggio has led Arizona Beverages to become one of the most recognized and beloved beverage brands in the world through his unique leadership style, business acumen, and innovative strategies. One of his key approaches is empowering his employees by fostering a culture of creativity and innovation. He encourages team members to share ideas and take ownership of their work, which not only boosts morale but also drives continuous improvement within the company. Open and honest communication is another cornerstone of Vultaggio's leadership style. By maintaining transparency with his team, he builds trust and ensures everyone is aligned with the company's goals and vision.

Additionally, Vultaggio's commitment to affordability and customer satisfaction has played a crucial role in Arizona's success. By maintaining a low price point of 99 cents for their large cans, the brand offers exceptional value, appealing to budget-conscious consumers without compromising on quality. Vultaggio actively listens to customer feedback, using it to guide product development and marketing strategies. This customer-centric approach fosters loyalty and ensures that the brand consistently meets consumer needs and expectations. Through these strategies, Don Vultaggio has established Arizona Beverages as a standout leader in the industry.

Don Vultaggio is a great leader because he empowers his employees, maintains transparent communication, and prioritizes customer satisfaction through innovative, value-driven strategies and you can see the impact of his great leadership in the success of his organisation.

Jamie Dimon Chairman and CEO of JPMorgan Chase

Jamie Dimon is widely regarded as one of the most influential and effective leaders in the financial industry. His exceptional financial acumen and strategic vision have been instrumental in steering the bank to its current position as a global leader. Under his leadership, JPMorgan Chase has not only expanded its market presence but also consistently delivered strong financial performance, even during periods of economic turbulence. Dimon's ability to anticipate market trends and adapt strategies accordingly has been a key factor in the bank's sustained success.

One of Dimon's notable strengths is his focus on innovation and risk management. Recognizing the rapidly changing landscape of the financial industry, he has championed the adoption of advanced technologies and digital solutions to enhance the bank's operations and customer experience. This forward-thinking approach has enabled JPMorgan Chase to stay ahead of competitors and meet the evolving needs of its clients. Additionally, Dimon's emphasis on robust risk management practices has helped the bank navigate through financial crises, such as the 2008 economic downturn, with resilience and stability.

Dimon's leadership is also characterized by a strong commitment to corporate responsibility and ethical standards. He has been a vocal advocate for regulatory reforms and has implemented policies that promote transparency and accountability within the organization. This commitment to ethical conduct has not only enhanced the bank's reputation but also fostered trust among clients, investors, and regulators. Dimon's focus on corporate responsibility extends to the bank's community initiatives, where he has supported various programs aimed at economic development, education, and workforce training.

Furthermore, Dimon places a high value on employee development and fostering a positive corporate culture. He believes in investing in the growth and well-being of the bank's employees, recognizing that a motivated and skilled workforce is essential for long-term success. Under his leadership,

JPMorgan Chase has implemented numerous initiatives to support employee development, diversity, and inclusion. This focus on creating an inclusive and supportive work environment has not only improved employee satisfaction but also contributed to the bank's overall performance.

Jamie Dimon's leadership at JPMorgan Chase is marked by his strategic vision, innovative approach, commitment to corporate responsibility, and dedication to employee development. These qualities have not only propelled the bank to new heights but also set a benchmark for leadership in the financial industry. Through his effective management and forward-thinking strategies, Dimon has solidified his reputation as a great leader and an influential figure in the global financial sector.

Jack Ma *Founder of Alibaba Group*

Jack Ma, the founder of Alibaba Group, is widely celebrated as a visionary leader whose innovative thinking and entrepreneurial spirit have revolutionized the e-commerce industry. Starting with a modest beginning, Ma's ability to foresee the potential of the internet and e-commerce in China laid the foundation for Alibaba's phenomenal growth. His relentless pursuit of his vision and his capacity to inspire others with his ideas have been instrumental in transforming Alibaba from a small start-up into a global conglomerate.

One of the hallmarks of Ma's leadership is his unwavering focus on customer satisfaction. He has always emphasized that the customer comes first, followed by employees, and then shareholders. This customer-centric approach has been pivotal in building Alibaba's reputation and fostering loyalty among its vast user base. By prioritizing customer needs and continuously innovating to improve their experience, Ma ensured that Alibaba stayed ahead of the curve in the highly competitive e-commerce landscape.

Jack Ma's leadership is also characterized by his commitment to fostering a culture of innovation and resilience. He encouraged a mindset that embraced failure as a learning opportunity, which empowered employees to take risks and think creatively. This culture of innovation has driven Alibaba's expansion into diverse areas such as cloud computing, digital payments, and artificial intelligence. Ma's ability to pivot and adapt to changing market dynamics has kept Alibaba at the forefront of technological advancements and industry trends.

Furthermore, Ma's dedication to social responsibility and philanthropy has set a strong example for corporate leadership. He has been a vocal advocate for using technology to address societal issues, such as poverty and education. Through the establishment of the Jack Ma Foundation, he has committed significant resources to initiatives aimed at improving education, supporting entrepreneurship, and addressing environmental challenges. His philanthropic efforts reflect his belief in giving back to society and making a positive impact on a global scale.

Jack Ma's leadership at Alibaba Group is distinguished by his visionary approach, customer-centric philosophy, commitment to innovation, and dedication to social responsibility. His ability to inspire and lead by example has not only propelled Alibaba to unprecedented success but also left a lasting impact on the global business landscape. Through his entrepreneurial journey and transformative leadership, Jack Ma has become a role model for aspiring entrepreneurs and business leaders worldwide.

Laura King: *A Transformative Leader at Clifford Chance*

Laura King, the Global Head of People and Talent at Clifford Chance, has established herself as a transformative leader through her innovative strategies and commitment to fostering an inclusive and supportive work environment. Her leadership has been pivotal in reshaping the firm's approach to talent management, ensuring that Clifford Chance remains competitive in attracting and retaining top legal talent globally.

Laura King's strategic vision for talent management encompasses a comprehensive approach to recruitment, development, and retention. She has implemented comprehensive programs that not only identify and attract high-calibre professionals but also nurture their growth within the firm. By focusing on continuous learning and development, King ensures that employees have the resources and opportunities to advance their skills and careers. Her initiatives in leadership development and mentoring have created a robust pipeline of future leaders within Clifford Chance.

A significant aspect of King's leadership is her unwavering commitment to diversity and inclusion. Recognizing the value of diverse perspectives in enhancing creativity and decision-making, she has championed policies and initiatives that promote inclusivity at all levels of the firm. Under her guidance, Clifford Chance has made substantial progress in creating a workplace where individuals from varied backgrounds feel valued and empowered. Her efforts include implementing diversity training, supporting affinity networks, and setting measurable goals for diversity and inclusion.

King's focus on employee engagement and well-being has been instrumental in building a positive organizational culture. She understands that a supportive work environment is crucial for employee satisfaction and productivity. To this end, she has introduced initiatives that address work-life balance, mental health, and overall well-being. By fostering open communication and providing resources for employee support, King has created a culture where employees feel heard and appreciated.

Laura King's leadership as the Global Head of People and Talent at Clifford Chance is marked by her visionary approach to talent management, her dedication to diversity and inclusion, her focus on employee engagement and well-being, and her innovative strategies in talent acquisition. Her comprehensive and forward-thinking initiatives have not only strengthened Clifford Chance's position as a leading global law firm but also set a benchmark for excellence in human resources leadership. Through her transformative leadership, Laura King has made a significant impact on the firm's culture, employee satisfaction, and overall success.

Dieter Zetsche: *A Visionary Leader at Daimler AG*

Dieter Zetsche, former Chairman of the Board of Management of Daimler AG and Head of Mercedes-Benz Cars, is celebrated for his transformative leadership and visionary approach in the automotive industry. Under his guidance, Daimler AG not only navigated through significant industry changes but also reinforced its position as a global leader in luxury automobiles.

Dieter Zetsche's tenure at Daimler AG was marked by a clear and strategic vision for the future of mobility. He foresaw the importance of innovation in maintaining a competitive edge and was instrumental in driving the company's focus towards sustainable and technologically advanced automotive solutions. This included pioneering efforts in electric mobility, autonomous driving, and connectivity, positioning Mercedes-Benz as a forward-thinking brand.

Zetsche championed the development of innovative technologies and new business models. Under his leadership, Daimler invested heavily in research and development, leading to breakthroughs in electric vehicle technology with the introduction of the EQ brand. His emphasis on innovation ensured that Mercedes-Benz remained at the forefront of the evolving automotive landscape.

One of Zetsche's key leadership qualities was his focus on empowering employees. He believed in fostering a culture of collaboration and inclusivity, where employees were encouraged to share ideas and contribute to the company's success. This approach not only boosted morale but also drove creativity and innovation within the organization.

Zetsche initiated significant cultural transformations at Daimler, breaking down traditional hierarchies and promoting a more agile and dynamic work environment. His efforts to modernize the corporate culture made the company more adaptable to change and better equipped to tackle future challenges.

Under Zetsche's leadership, Daimler AG took significant steps towards sustainability. He championed the development of eco-friendly vehicles and implemented sustainable practices across the company's operations. This commitment to environmental responsibility resonated with consumers and stakeholders alike, reinforcing the brand's image as a leader in sustainability.

Zetsche's leadership was characterized by resilience and adaptability. He successfully guided Daimler AG through various economic downturns and industry disruptions, ensuring the company's stability and growth. His ability to adapt to changing market conditions and pivot strategies as needed was crucial in maintaining Daimler's competitive edge.

Zetsche's long-term vision for Daimler included preparing the company for future mobility trends. By investing in electric vehicles, autonomous driving technology, and digital services, he positioned Daimler to thrive in the rapidly evolving automotive industry.

Dieter Zetsche's leadership at Daimler AG is marked by his visionary approach, commitment to innovation, and focus on empowering employees. His strategic vision and customer-centric mindset propelled Mercedes-Benz to new heights, while his emphasis on sustainability and corporate culture transformation ensured the company's long-term success. Through his effective management and forward-thinking strategies, Zetsche has left a legacy in the automotive industry as a great leader.

Further Reading

Finally, to be a great manager and leader, you need to find greatness within yourself. Working on yourself is key—recognize your strengths, embrace your potential, and continuously strive for personal and professional growth. This journey of self-improvement and self-discovery will inspire those around you and pave the way for true leadership.

Here is a list of my personal list of books that I would recommend for self-help and growth that should transform you into a better leader:

The 7 Habits of Highly Effective People" by Stephen R. Covey

- "Never Eat Alone" by Keith Ferrazzi

- How to Win Friends and Influence People" by Dale Carnegie

- "The Power of Now: A Guide to Spiritual Enlightenment" by Eckhart Tolle

- "Rich Dad Poor Dad" by Robert Kiyosaki

- "The 48 Laws of Power" by Robert Greene

- "The Subtle Art of Not Giving a F*ck" by Mark Manson

- "The First 90 Days" by Michael Watkins

- "The Prince" by Niccolo Machiavelli

- "7 Habits of Highly Effective People" by Stephen R. Covey

www.ingramcontent.com/pod-product-compliance
Lightning Source LLC
Chambersburg PA
CBHW071954210526
45479CB00003B/935